A PAGEANT OF BRITISH STEAM

STEAM PRESERVATION IN THE 21ST CENTURY

A PAGEANT OF BRITISH STEAM

STEAM PRESERVATION IN THE 21ST CENTURY

Geoff Swaine

PEN & SWORD
TRANSPORT

AN IMPRINT OF PEN & SWORD BOOKS LTD.
YORKSHIRE – PHILADELPHIA

First published in Great Britain in 2018 by
Pen and Sword Transport

An imprint of
Pen & Sword Books Ltd
Yorkshire - Philadelphia

ISBN 978 1 52671 757 3

Typeset by Aura Technology and Software Services, India.
Printed and bound by Replika Press Pvt. Ltd.

Pen & Sword Books Ltd incorporates the Imprints of Pen & Sword
Books Archaeology, Atlas, Aviation, Battleground, Discovery, Family History,
History, Maritime, Military, Naval, Politics, Railways, Select, Transport,
True Crime, Fiction, Frontline Books, Leo Cooper, Praetorian Press,
Seaforth Publishing, Wharncliffe and White Owl.

For a complete list of Pen & Sword titles please contact
PEN & SWORD BOOKS LIMITED
47 Church Street, Barnsley, South Yorkshire, S70 2AS, England
E-mail: enquiries@pen-and-sword.co.uk
Website: www.pen-and-sword.co.uk

or

PEN AND SWORD BOOKS
1950 Lawrence Rd, Havertown, PA 19083, USA
E-mail: Uspen-and-sword@casematepublishers.com
Website: www.penandswordbooks.com

CONTENTS

INTRODUCTION

Above: 4-6-2 LMS No. 6201 *Princess Elizabeth* set a steam record for the 401 mile Glasgow to London run in 1936 at an average speed of 70mph. An incredible achievement, especially considering the summits which had to be overcome. Here the Pacific engine takes a railtour past Bishops Stortford in Essex heading for Norwich.

Left: Following a ten year overhaul, No. 60103 *Flying Scotsman* makes appearances all across the country. Here the popular engine can be seen on the Bluebell Railway heading a northbound service towards East Grinstead.

In the guise of 92220 *Evening Star* at Loughborough is BS '9F' 2-10-0 No.92214, a descendant from the Riddles wartime design with the same wheel arrangement.

The classic LMS 'Duchess' makes a visit to the Tyseley summer open day as a guest visitor to this GWR stronghold. LMS 'Coronation' Class '8P' 4-6-2 No. 46233 *Duchess of Sutherland* leads the cavalcade.

Above: Built by Bulleid for the Southern Railway, air-smoothed Pacific *City of Wells* crosses the River Irwell on the East Lancs Railway.

Left: BR No. 34092 'West Country' Pacific *City of Wells* at Rawtenstall, the northern end of the East Lancs Railway. Pacific is the name given to any locomotive with a 4-6-2 wheel arrangement.

The preserved railways of Britain have risen in half a century to become an industrial wonder of the world. After the Second World War, Britain continued with steam power for railways because the nation was literally bankrupt and could not afford the cost of importing diesel fuel. An abundant supply of coal was still there to be mined, so the government decreed that the country should advance forward with steam power. This was unlike other nations of Europe who had their railway systems virtually wiped out. For them, almost a complete rebuild was necessary, which would go forward with diesel and electric traction. To support the decision to proceed with steam, the British Government ordered twelve classes of new locomotives of which 999 were built.

The continuing of steam through the 1950s led to a whole new pastime evolving – trainspotting. The lads had their Ian Allan spotters' books which listed every single locomotive, giving their wheel arrangement, power rating and even their shed allocation. The wonder of all this was to come to an end though; in 1955, the British Transport Commission issued a document stating that within a decade all steam power would be removed from the railways, to be replaced by diesel and electric traction.

This operation proceeded in a confused manner, for while the Commission attempted to remove steam, British Railways were still building their range of Standard Class steam locomotives, a situation which carried on right up to 1960.

To speed up the railway rationalisation, an industrialist was employed to oversee the Modernisation Plan and make some recommendations. His name was Dr Richard Beeching, who issued his report in 1963. This report showed, that in his opinion, 5,000 miles of railway lines should be removed, 2,000 stations shut down and all steam power removed, taking with it all the sheds and paraphernalia which supported the steam industry. Oh, and also thousands of rail jobs would go, leaving many men who had family traditions in the railways without employment. As could be imagined, the name Beeching became notorious in a nation who loved industry and steam power. The Beeching Plan was put into operation, with his full closure plan being achieved by 1973.

It is true that Britain had too many railway lines. In Victorian times, the railway mania was being led by private industrialists, whose only thoughts were in capital gain. The government and population of the day were all caught up in the wonder of the new transport system and how for the first time the ordinary person could travel beyond the confines of their own town or village. Rail lines went to the coast, thereby making holidays available for the first time. At the time all those coastal places were just little villages and hamlets. Once the railways arrived they grew to become the resorts they are today.

Likewise, industry was caught up in it all. Cotton could be delivered in hours to the inland mills rather than days by canal. Coal could be delivered to all the industry which needed it. The residents of inland towns could eat fresh fish for the first time with the product reaching them the same day it arrived in the ports.

The fast and almost uncontrolled expansion of the railways in the 1800s led to many routes being duplicated, with many towns being served by more than one private railway company. This didn't happen in the other countries of Europe, as those systems were generally government planned, whereby the end product was ordered and methodically produced. A century later, the duplication of lines in Britain did prove to have an advantage because in wartime, when the railways were targeted by bombs, it often turned out that there was an alternative route not very far away.

It is true that the steam engines had to go at some time. In the 1950s, there was inadequate manpower to clean and maintain them. Effectively, a generation had been lost to the war, with most of the new kids coming through being unwilling to take on the job of cleaning locomotives. After the war, the rail system was in a totally dilapidated state which carried on right through the Fifties. Even the new engines quickly became covered in grime, which would never be removed.

The lads who were interested in trains, which was most of them, still loved everything about steam. They were horrified that locomotives being built in the late Fifties were destined to be scrapped within five years of their manufacture, a total waste of something which should have a life of some thirty years.

The situation led to the young – and not so young – trying to buy some of these locomotives. The only problem was finding somewhere to put them. It soon became very obvious that the ideal place would be one of those branch lines which Beeching closed. It first happened in Sussex, where a short stretch of track between two stations had not yet been lifted. A small group of people did manage to buy a lease on it and start it up as a preserved railway. This developed into the Bluebell Railway. A couple of narrow-gauge lines in Wales had shown the way, so it could be done. After all, British Railways had no use for disused branch lines. Many others followed quickly, leading to the evolvement of a Preservation Movement. By the turn of the century, these heritage lines totalled over a hundred, giving us a new leisure industry which satisfies in every way the love for steam power. In the depths of an over-zealous closure plan devised by Dr. Beeching, we have obtained an unbelievable preserved railway system which is quite unlike anything else in the world.

CHAPTER 1

EARLIEST DAYS

830 can be considered to be Year 1 in the history of passenger travel on the railways. To get to this point there had to be nearly thirty years of development since Richard Trevithick came up with a steam locomotive which could propel itself. Before that, there was a good century of development regarding stationary steam engines.

The Stockton and Darlington event of 1825 had proved the experiment that people could be hauled by an engine along a track – but that was a one-off. Also, there had been the Rainhill Trials of 1829 when a competition had established the best design of a locomotive with which to go forward. However, it was the Liverpool & Manchester Railway, on the same tracks as the Rainhill Trials, which produced a timetabled railway service between two places for the first time. The building of this railway was instigated by the businessmen of Liverpool who could see the need to supply the burgeoning mills of Manchester with the raw cotton to keep them going.

The expansion of the railways in the 1830s revitalised the nation's economy. It brought the country out of the depressed times of the decade before. A transport revolution had emerged to provide new opportunities and industrial wealth. The energy of the Industrial Revolution was rekindled. The whole nation became caught up with this new-found freedom of movement, with farm workers vacating the land for a perceived better life in the ever-expanding cities. The newly emerging middle classes also could be part of it by buying shares in the railways.

The need for new money to feed the expansion led to the privately-owned companies offering share floats, at prices which for the first time were at a level which the lower classes could afford. Great railway centres emerged such as Crewe, Swindon and Derby, creating the bases for manufacturing steam locomotives and associated products. All areas wanted some of the railway action and there were entrepreneurs and business men to provide it.

A whole change to people's lives was happening. Not only did it give the opportunity to travel, but aspects of life were improved by the supply of goods and food items. The supply of coal to the big cities provided a new widespread heating source. Iron ore, minerals, bulk goods as well as livestock could now be transported to all areas. Livestock could be moved, doing away with the need to herd them for hundreds of miles 'on the hoof', all leading to ever improving lifestyles.

By 1838, Birmingham had linked to London. Soon the capital was becoming the hub of it all, with rail companies anxious to get a link and take advantage of the capital's need for commodities.

The Liverpool to Manchester Railway(L&M) had opened for passengers in 1830. It was the first ever passenger railway in the world linking two cities. At Liverpool, trucks from Lime Street station could be cable-hauled to link with the trains at Edge Hill. City dwellers were suspicious of these fiery monsters coming too close to home. The demand to travel on the L&M was immense, with people travelling miles just to watch it from the sidelines; it was an event of awe and wonder. Construction had also to break new ground with the Sankey viaduct and the ground-breaking support construction over Chat Moss, the big area of bog near Eccles. A huge amount of tunnelling and rock-blasting was necessary at Olive Mount and the further approaches to Liverpool.

This was a new surge in the Industrial Revolution, whereby the canals of the previous century slowly gave way to this new and more speedy form of transport. Through the 1830s, every aspect to do with railways was learning and improving. Locomotives, rails, signalling and safety aspects were continually being improved. Stations had no platforms to begin with, passengers boarding a train from ground level as they would a stage coach.

The locomotive *Planet* had been developed by Robert Stephenson for passenger traffic and this became the yardstick upon which all locomotive manufacturers would base their designs. The L&M track was still laid on concrete blocks, although no horses were ever used on the line. The concrete blocks had become the norm for all railway construction until 1837, a design which had been devised for horses, allowing them to walk between the rails whilst pulling the trucks. All rails were then of the fish-bellied type, with now a heavier section coming in. Rails had improved vastly since wrought iron had been developed in Northumberland in 1820, which replaced the former brittle cast iron rails which were used before that date.

By 1837, heavier sections of wrought iron rails were needed to carry new breeds of engine. Also, it was found that timber sleepers prevented any tendency for tracks to spread therefore allowing for the heavier loads and higher speeds. This meant that train speeds could be increased from the limit of 17mph, to over 30mph. It would not be until 1857 that steel rails replaced wrought iron, again allowing higher speeds to be permitted.

Signalling was virtually non-existent through the 1830s. Train movement relied on policemen, dressed in a frock coat and a stove-pipe hat. They had to let a train through a section with hand signals after a time limit had elapsed. Usually they allowed a period of six minutes before signalling another one forward. There was absolutely no knowledge or indication if the train in front had cleared the section, hence accidents were commonplace.

The invention of the electric telegraph in 1838 was to help save the day. After this development, a one needle indicator could be placed in each of the police-man's huts joined by a wire to the next one. He could indicate to the man at the next section once a train had entered the section and get a reverse signal back when the train had passed through. A turning disc signal on a pole would indicate to the train driver if he had a clear road ahead. Variations on this system carried the railways through the next decade. Semaphore signals soon came in, allowing much clearer information to the drivers and hence again making faster speeds possible. At first, all the apparatus was out in the open before signal boxes came in with their much more elaborate safety systems.

The 1830s was a period of experimentation, to learn by experience especially after an accident. The railways had taken off as a mode of transport which the public loved. Lifestyles were to change dramatically.

Replica *Rocket* heads towards Loughborough on the Great Central Railway.

Richard Trevithick built the original loco *Catch Me Who Can* in 1808 at the Hazledine Foundry of Bridgnorth. Now, 200 years later, some local enthusiasts show off their rebuild, also at Bridgnorth. The original was the first engine to pull fare-paying passengers on a circular track in London, but unfortunately it broke the cast-iron rails.

A cut-away version Replica *Rocket* is on display in the Main Hall of the National Railway Museum.

Above: A railway carriage had to be invented from scratch, so carriage-makers just placed stagecoach styled units onto a frame. The frame would have been that of an existing goods wagon. Early passengers mounted the coach from ground level – just as they would boarding a stage coach.

Right: Replica engine *Planet* emerges from its home at the Manchester Museum of Science to pull in to Liverpool Road station, the start of the Manchester to Liverpool railway. The home of the Rainhill Trials and the first ever line on which a steam passenger railway ran.

On loan from the Manchester Museum of Science, replica engine *Planet* is making an appearance at the Great Central Railway in Leicestershire. The original *Planet* was built by Robert Stephenson in 1830 for service on the Manchester to Liverpool line.

Above: Furness No. 20 stands by at Loughborough Central waiting for her next duty on the preserved main line. In Indian Red livery, No. 20 is Britain's oldest working standard gauge locomotive and was restored to working life in 1999 by the Furness Railway Trust.

Right: The replica broad gauge engine *Fire Fly* emerges from the Didcot transfer shed to perform a turn of duty on the Didcot dual-gauge demonstration line. 1840 technology has been recreated at Didcot.

Left: Broad gauge replica *Fire Fly* advances from the transfer shed with her demonstration train at the Didcot Railway Centre. In the background is the former Frome Mineral Junction signalbox.

Below: 2-2-2 *Fire Fly* stands on the broad-gauge section of line. Visitors can get very close to admire this reproduced vision of the past.

Hundreds of little railway companies had joined the railway bandwagon by the 1840s, all taking advantage of the government's easy attitude for passing proposals brought before Parliament. Governments of the time only stepped in where safety was an issue, or if the needs of the working people were not being accommodated. With such ease were new lines given permission to go ahead, that duplication became commonplace.

The railway's expansion was like the internet expansion of a hundred and fifty years later where a surge was created, making people's lives better and easier. The ordinary working person had freedom of movement for the first time. A market town may have been ten miles away, but before the coming of these railway track`s, the only option most people had to get to the market town was on foot. The ordinary person would be well used to walking considerable distances. A few may have had access to a horse, but that was the way to get around then – on foot. Hence most of the town and village dwellers never ventured further than the next town in their lives.

Private rail companies became established, all seeking to own railways for their own gain. To finance this, share issues were offered, offering returns which could not be obtained elsewhere. For the first time, shares became within reach of the ordinary working person. A newly emerging middle class bought these in abundance to finance their ever-improving lifestyle. It was all on a roll, which, to the owners, workers and shareholders, looked as if it would go on for ever.

Large numbers of these small railway companies linked with others in takeovers and amalgamations and the country suddenly found it had a rail network. They all loved it, and bought into it. Wealth and mobility; what more could they want? Mania had set in, which today we would recognise as a bubble; but they didn't. In 1846, 272 Acts of Parliament were passed for new railways or extensions to existing ones. Thousands of miles of track were added to the country's map, again many duplicating existing services. Nobody seemed to mind; the duplication led to different companies sharing the same station. Three used Derby and four different companies ran through Chester. Many towns had more than one station where sharing a station was frowned upon.

Lines leading towards London became duplicated, which, with competition, led to reduced fares. This tendency had the result of lowering dividends being offered to shareholders as the companies ran short of cash. Financiers such as George Hudson had been building an empire, buying out everything he needed to get from Yorkshire and the Midlands to London. The Great Western Railway, having completed their flagship line from London to Bristol, expanded right though the south-west and Wales.

Big stations were also deemed to be the right thing for the ends of the line in the big cities. The mighty Brunel had laid down plans for a new structure in London. His opulent outlook was copied by others, the owners wanting their legacy to stand after them. The ones which had been bought out had taken their profit, leaving those remaining to project and chart their future assumed profits and wealth.

However, in 1846, the government felt the over-heating economy needed to be adjusted and increased interest rates. The railway-mania, could not be sustained and just as quickly as they all had wanted to buy shares, there was now a stampede to sell them. The bubble had burst. People who had invested their life savings lost everything; they had bought shares under schemes where they didn't need to pay everything up front. Rail owners quickly went bankrupt. George Hudson, the man who had laid down the network of the Midland Railway was one of them; he lost everything. With something like the railways, the owners and shareholders may have gone bust, but the rail network they created was still there. The people had their railways and wanted to keep using them. It was time for the government to take a bit more interest to help sort out the mess. What resulted was that the more sensibly-run companies of the past could be given the chance to take over and continue with a more regulated system.

With the ordinary person having to work six days a week and attending church on Sunday, the only time to make a rail journey would be on Sunday afternoons. With this in mind, many of the early excursions were linked to the church. The originator of the famous travel company Thomas Cook started this way. He organised excursions from Leicester on a Sunday for followers to attend a religious gathering in Loughborough eleven miles away. This is, of course, the present route of the preserved Great Central Railway.

With the designing and building of a major railroad, and there were so many of these being built at the time, it was essential to find the most economical route in regard to terrain. If you were lucky it could be all about crossing flatlands or following a river valley. But the alternative was to go against the grain and have to cross one river valley after another. This meant one thing – viaducts; a very expensive item. This was all new ground, for there was very little previous knowledge as to the design and construction. An engineer could not provide calculations to suit potential loadings, or the forces on the structure of a train crossing one. The end result was that they were built super-strong, which benefits us today because they mostly all still stand, to do a job for the advanced trains of now. We can marvel at their quality, the design and workmanship of these structures. For if one becomes part of a redundant railway, it is rarely pulled down.

The Transfer Shed at the Didcot Railway Centre. An original building where goods from one gauge would be transferred to the train of the other. On the left is original standard gauge steam Railcar No. 93. While on the right is the replica broad gauge loco *Fire Fly*. The shed dates from 1863 and was rescued from another part of Didcot.

Above: The perfect sight on a Southern steam heritage railway is the Stroudley 'Terrier' tank loco. Looking splendid in authentic green livery, ex-LBSCR No. 8 *Freshwater* switches platforms at Havenstreet, Isle of Wight.

Right: One of the most enduring locos ever is the diminutive Stroudly 'Terrier'. No. 32678 pulls away from Tenterden on the Kent & East Sussex Railway. The class originally hauled early commuter trains around south and east London. Many survive to this day, proving how successful they were.

Above: In steam at Tenterden in Kent is tank loco 0-6-0ST *Charwelton*. The 1917 built Manning Wardle shunter is turned out in the immaculate original umber livery of its first employer – the Parkgate Iron & Steel Company of Charwelton.

Left: Broad gauge and standard gauge trains rode the same dual-gauge track before the broad gauge disappeared in 1892. Note the variety of early signaling here at Didcot.

CHAPTER 2

LATE VICTORIAN PROGRESS

By this time, we were some sixty years into railway development. All through the decades momentum had kept going with the mode of transport being recognised as the changer of people's lives – for the better. All the major towns and cities had stations to be proud of. The biggest being cathedrals to the railway with the smaller ones having a proud look about them. The more important a town seemed to be, the more important did the station look.

In the years since the start of the railways, innovations had been made, everyone learning by their experiences, for there were no previous guidelines to learn from, the scientists being every inch as important as the men on the ground. The workings of a steam engine are a science lesson in their own right.

Nearly all parts of the country had become served by railways. Some remote areas had been unlucky – so far. But in 1896, the government approved the 'Light Railways Act' with the aim to encourage the building of lines to these remote areas. This led people such as Colonel Stephens to build multiple small lines across the country. One of these being the Kent & East Sussex Railway which is such a creditable part of our heritage scene.

Aspects of railway infrastructure such as rails, points, signalling and operations of services had developed so far that faster speeds could be obtained. Bogies had been added to carriages enabling them to be longer and more comfortable. All this led to the need for locomotives to become bigger. Speed suddenly became the in thing, with the newspapers reporting everything new. Faster times between major cities were always newsworthy with the coming of new 'speedy' engines such as the *Stirling Single* hitting the newsprint. Of course, it was the railways which carried the newspapers to their morning destinations, a facility which had established the coming of the national dailies. They all loved railway stories for it was to that mode of transport that they owed their existence. They did notice that a certain amount of competition was happening where two railways could cover a particular service.

The bringing of trans-Atlantic boat passengers from Plymouth to London had led to great competition between the L&SWR and GWR, both wishing to collar this lucrative trade, with the greatest and most publicised rivalry taking in the competition from London to Scotland, so much so that the 'Races to the North' became a national intrigue.

The Great Northern Railway led the way from King's Cross, passing over to the North Eastern who had running rights to Edinburgh. This was the east-coast route, with the rival west-coast route being headed by the L&NWR and the Caledonian from Carlisle. In the early 1890s, the time taken for the journeys was ten hours for the west coast and nine for the east, averaging around 40-43mph. During two summers in the mid-1890s it all came to a head.

Both routes had a 10.00am start from London and both had an evening departure to Aberdeen which became the better focus for the racing. Both would get to their core destinations of Glasgow and Edinburgh before departing for the final leg, which had one great point of interest; as they were heading to Aberdeen, the last part of that route was single tracked. Therefore, whoever got to the point of Kinnaber Junction, some 36 miles short of Aberdeen, first was the certain winner; they would be led onto the single track with the loser having no option but to creep along behind in second place.

The railways had shrunk the country, with times to Edinburgh being reduced from ten hours in 1869 to six hours in 1936. This was when LMS No. 6201 *Princess Elizabeth* achieved this time on a 401-mile southbound run on the west-coast side. All the time, great breakthroughs were being made which improved the quality and enjoyment of rail travel for the public.

Breakthroughs were being made in every department in the late 1890s, the lighting of carriages being a prime example. In those early wooden-bodied carriages, the lighting consisted of oil and then oil-gas and traditional gas, housed in iron cylinders slung beneath the carriage; an explosive situation and fire hazard at the best of times. Oil lighting stayed in some capacity through until the 1930s although by the turn of the century, battery and dynamo powered electric light had come in; a huge improvement and one which the Edwardians exploited to the full in their improvements of the rail product. The last decade of the century also led to steam heating being introduced to carriages. This was after experimentation with some primitive foot-warming devices.

The biggest innovation, and one which led to much more comfort as well as higher speeds for the trains, was the introduction of bogies to the coaches. These are the four-wheeled sets beneath the carriage ends which swivel independently to the structure above and it spelled the end for the rigid four and six wheels which had served the railways in their formative years. Carriages became bigger with a corridor link alongside the compartments being very useful, because accessible toilets then enabled trains to travel longer distances, eliminating the need for comfort stops. Continuous fitted brakes, lighting, heating and upholstered seats added so much more to the travelling experience giving the public the ever-improving service they desired.

Carriages became bigger and heavier, carrying many more passengers; hence there was the continuous need to build more powerful steam locomotives. All cities expanded their suburban rail systems, the introduction of larger tank engines becoming necessary. Movement of large numbers of passengers over relatively short distances removed the needs for luxuries such as corridors or lavatories. The poor souls were packed in sometimes with seven a side seated and a further half dozen standing in one compartment. Not a pleasant experience, especially as smoking was also allowed in some compartments.

Railways allowed sport to excel, for now players and spectators could travel the same tracks to get to far off places which were previously out of reach. Classes could also mix for it was only in sport that they did so. National leagues emerged in football, cricket and other sports to a lesser extent. Horse racing also became very popular, because the horses could travel by train also. A whole new way of taking up leisure time emerged growing ever bigger and more popular. The newspapers reporting it and loving it.

History has told us that the Edwardian period was known as a 'Golden Age' for Britain's railways. The trials and errors of the Victorian age had been ironed out. Locomotion, tracks and carriages had improved to such an extent that the public revelled in the glory of it all. Everything gleamed in polished wood and fine paintwork all buffed up and used with pride.

It takes much muscle power to turn an engine at Keighley. Fortunately the loco on the turntable is the lightweight Hudswell Clarke engine *Nunlow*. Built in 1938 for use at G&T Earles cement works at Hope, Derbyshire.

Right: No. 1704 *Nunlow* earns her keep and proves her power by taking a service out of Keighley station to attack the rise to Ingrow.

Below: ex-SECR 'C' Class No. 592 (BR 31592) awaits the guard's signal to blow her whistle and take the train off towards East Grinstead on the Bluebell Railway.

Through Edwardian times, and especially into the Twenties, the increased demand on suburban services called for larger tank engines to be built. For the GNR No.1744 came off the production line in 1920 and the 'N2' is showing authentic pre-grouping livery.

Another large tank engine built for the LNER, here seen in North Norfolk, is 'N7' No. (BR) 69621. This was a class which proved more than capable in operating an intensive timetable out of London's Liverpool Street station in the 1920s.

Above: A sight which would have made a railway official cry in the sixties – a diesel multiple unit (the new pride of the railways) being pulled by a steam engine. Here, the ever-roving Port Talbot Railway 0-6-0ST No. 813 looks splendid in the evening sunshine at Bury.

Right: SE&CR 0-4-4T No.263 in action at Horstead Keynes on the Bluebell Railway, Ashford built in 1905.

'Dukedog' *Earl of Berkeley* has the early BR mixed traffic livery of black with the lion and wheel logo on the tender.

City of Truro on show at Toddington showing her fine Edwardian livery.

The Auto-train makes a splendid sight having just left Glyndyfrdwy and heading upgrade towards Berwyn tunnel. The driver controls the regulator in the engine by means of rods carried below the train. The maximum range of these rods is usually two carriages.

An Auto-train takes water halfway up the platform owing to its formation as a push-pull unit. A classic view of Llangollen station from the medieval bridge across the River Dee.

The engine of the Auto-train is Class '6400' Pannier tank No. 6430. Note how the engine is finished in fully lined Brunswick Green. This is the livery generally attributed to the Western Region express locomotives.

Steam Railmotor No. 93 prepares to make another run down the line to Brentford and back from Southall.

The Steam Railmotor adds water to its 400 gallon tank in readiness for the next journey. Note the bags of coal on the platform.

Robinson 2-8-0 No. 63601 was the type the engine selected by the Ministry of Supply to be the mainstay loco-type to be produced en masse for the First World War. Here the only example in Britain waits out of service at Loughborough.

Right: 2-8-0 No. 63601 picks up speed out of Loughborough as she heads down the double track section of the Great Central Railway.

Below: 'Railway Operating Division' (ROD) '43xx' Class 2-6-0 No. 5322 was built in 1917. Given the ROD identity, she was shipped to France for war use from new. In the Great War even the engines had to wear khaki.

ROD No. 5322 makes a fine sight on the Didcot express line.

From a design conceived in the century before, this inside cylindered 'J15' was built at Stratford in 1912. The engine carried numbers LNER 7564 & BR 65462 before withdrawal in 1962. Here it climbs the bank out of Sheringham in North Norfolk.

Above: Midland Railway '4F' 0-6-0 No. 43924 teams up with L&NWR 'Coal Tank' No. 1054 for a run up the line with the next service.

Left: The only survivor of a class which worked the mineral trains around Consett. 'Q6' 0-8-0 No. 63395 climbs the notorious 1 in 49 gradient into Goathland station on the North Yorkshire Moors Railway, not too difficult in mid-summer with this great surviving engine.

CHAPTER 3

THE BIG FOUR

Above: Steaming out of Bury Bolton St station and into the evening sunshine is 'Crab' LMS 5MT 2-6-0 No. 13065 (BR 42765). All the great engines of the LMS carried the fabulous crimson-lake livery at one time or another.

Right: Resident at the Kent & East Sussex Railway is GWR (WR) Pannier Tank '16xx' Class 0-6-0T No. 1638. Regarded as by many to be the best tank engine ever, these Panniers readily perform all duties on a railway. One of the later variations built at Swindon in 1949.

Thompson 'B1' 4-6-0 No. 61306 on the Battlefield Line in Leicestershire. Being built in 1948 the engine went straight into British Railways service. Former liveries could be applied for a couple of years until BR settled on its own Blackberry black. No. 61306 is carrying the LNER livery of lined apple green.

The SR 'Schools' were a highly successful engine named after Public Schools. Forty were built with three surviving into preservation. Built from 1930 with the width restrictions on the London to Hastings line in mind, Maunsell took a chance on the 4-4-0 wheel arrangement, but they did very well. No. 30925 *Cheltenham* is working the Great Central main line.

Through the Edwardian period, hundreds of private railway companies had been set up to be part of the system. Mergers and takeovers enabled the network to emerge with long-distance services being available. Where there wasn't a takeover, running rights would be obtained over someone else's lines for the key long-distance journeys to be completed. Even after the First World War, when the government wanted to pass the railways back to the private ownership, there were still some 120 potential operators. Needless to say, they were not all pleased with taking back what was being offered, a run down and neglected set of track and infrastructure ravaged by the war operations. All the colour and cheerfulness of the Edwardian period had disappeared.

The government had to rationalise things, and while nationalisation was considered, it was not thought to be the path forward. What was, was the restructuring of everything to be run by just four private companies – one for each region. It was a procedure which commonly became known as 'Grouping'. The four companies would be, the Southern Railway, Great Western Railway (which was largely unchanged from before, although extended), London & North Eastern Railway and London Midland & Scottish Railway, the largest of them all – still being the legacy of George Hudson. There were a very few small companies who were allowed to continue such as the Midland & Great Northern, Somerset and Dorset Railway etc.

The Southern Railway incorporated three constituents in the south and south-west. LMS took over those companies serving the Midlands and West Coast route leading into Scotland. The LNER took care of the eastern side, with the East Coast route leading into many parts of Scotland, Scotland's old companies such as the Caledonian, Highland and North British being absorbed.

The 'Big Four' companies had their legality established by the Railways Act of 1921 to come into being on 1 January 1923. Each company had a Chief Mechanical Engineer (CME), a person with wide ranging powers, especially in the design of their locomotives and rolling stock. These men became famous with the legacy of their famous engines always being referenced back to them. In those early days, the LMS had Hughes and Fowler; the LNER had Gresley; the GWR had Collett who took over from the great G.J. Churchward; the Southern took on the former South Eastern & Chatham man, Richard Maunsell.

We were, by this time, three generations into the railways and a rigid hierarchy stood at every Railway Centre. For someone to be promoted into a top railway position, the man in situ would have to either retire or die. It was often the way that the present top man would have nurtured his successor as his number two for a number of years. Likewise, railway jobs in the factories or out in the running sections were highly sought after. Usually, it was the sons of railwaymen who got first chance at apprenticeships or to fill any other sought-after jobs.

The CMEs firstly had to assess what they had inherited, as many engines were coming through from earlier contracts where orders had been placed. Midland policy had been to build high numbers of medium powered locos always with the idea of doubling up when there was a heavy load. Whereas the Great Northern had already stated their case with the 'A1s' coming through, the Great Western were adapting their 'Star' class into becoming 'Castles' – the Southern always had their eye on electrification.

The 1930s were the times of the Great Depression which severely set back the public and their spending power. However, the government of the time did throw large amounts of money at the railways, with the intention of doing something to lift the nation. That they certainly did, because we came into one of the most exciting periods in railway history – the age of the Streamliner.

Nigel Gresley had powered ahead with his large engines. No. 4472 of the 'A1' Class (later to be 'A3'), *Flying Scotsman*, had in 1928 become the first engine to take a train non-stop from London to Edinburgh.

Henry Fowler had taken over on the LMS to supervise construction of the 2-6-0 'Crabs' which were a great success, but again only had the 5MT power rating. From 1932, William Stanier was recruited from the GWR by the LMS for one thing; transform the company and allow it to compete with the LNER with the introduction of new classes of big engines and also to find a locomotive which could make the Euston to Glasgow journey without changing engines. Previously, it was largely the 'Royal Scots' which had been performing this task. With their 7MP they ran just that bit short and had to be changed at Carlisle.

Stanier certainly did this; before very long, the 'Princess Royal' Class (8MT) appeared, thirteen of which came through the Crewe works between 1933 and 1935.

All bearing names, they were the largest engines of the time. With a massive boiler and formidable appearance, there was also a huge firegrate totalling 45sq ft. LMS 4-6-2 No. 6201 *Princess Elizabeth* set a steam record for the 401 mile Glasgow to London run in 1936 at an average speed of 70mph, an incredible achievement, especially considering the Shap and Beattock summits which had to be overcome. As well as the great 'Black 5s' and '8Fs', the 'Jubilees' came onto the scene between 1934 and 1936, followed by the classic 'Princess Coronation' class (the 'Duchesses') from 1937.

Gresley didn't miss out, for he produced the greatest of them all. With his Pacific 'A4s', he had an engine which would take the world speed record for a steam engine. On 3 July 1938, No. 4468 (BR 60022) *Mallard* hauled a train down the Stoke Bank near Peterborough at an incredible 126mph (202.7km/h). We were back into the fast runs to Scotland, and into the coming age of streamlining.

The Southern Railway didn't miss out either, as Maunsell produced a 4-cylinder 4-6-0 'Lord Nelson' class, which he claimed to be more powerful than the GWR equivalent – the 'Castles'. This put the wind up Swindon and they responded by producing as much power as could be put onto a frame of a 4-6-0 engine. Very soon the 'Kings' were to be wheeled out.

All this excitement went on through the rest of the Thirties until the country was hit for the second time within a generation by war.

When war broke out again, the Chief Mechanical Engineers of the four railway companies were: Sir Nigel Gresley of the LNER; William Stanier for the LMS; Collett for the GWR; and Oliver Bulleid for the Southern, having taken over from Maunsell in 1937. Gresley was to survive only until 1941 when Edward Thompson filled that post. Thompson, though, was only to last until 1946 when Peppercorn became the main man.

All these railways had been given back their control by the government after wartime, although the condition of these was nothing like that which had been handed over in 1939. The government handover came with a directive – build more engines and quickly. Bulleid continued with his 'Merchant Navy' types, also introducing the 'Light Pacifics' with the 'West Country' and 'Battle of Britain Classes'. Hawksworth came up with the 'Counties' and 'Modified Halls' together with building more 'Castles' and 'Manors'. George Ivatt and Fairburn were late incumbents for the LMS and they both have legacies which can be still seen in preservation.

Peppercorn continued with some of the Gresley ideas. A plan to develop the 'K4' Class (of which an example *The Great Marquess* has been preserved) into a new 3-cylinder type was progressed – just six of these were built. The 'K1s' which had the 'Utility Front' indicates how austerity was still at the forefront. The Thompson 'B1' was successful with orders being placed for further batches. Thompson had also designed the 'A2s', as there was now a shortage of express passenger engines, but with limited success. However, Peppercorn did get it right with one of his developments, the 'A1s'. Fifty Peppercorn 'A1s' came off the production line in the late 1940s, none being saved for the nation. A group of preservationists put this right, for in 2008 for they wheeled out a brand new one, built from scratch – No. 60163 *Tornado*.

Nationalisation was deemed to be the answer for the woes of the transport system and on 1 January 1948 it all went into national ownership. Britain had to continue with coal firing, and a new set of locomotives was planned. But all evidence showed that the last decades of steam were coming upon us.

CHAPTER 4

SOUTHERN SPECIALS

The only surviving example of the Urie designed 'N15' LSWR Class. The design was taken further by Maunsell for the Southern Railway and called 'King Arthurs' - used for express passenger work. No. 30777 *Sir Lamiel* is seen here in Brunswick Green livery outside the Loughborough works.

Above: A typical Southern Railway steam locomotive is No. 847 S Class. U Class 2-6-0 from 1936. One of Maunsell's Moguls based on a design by Urie of the L&SWR before the 'Grouping' of 1923. It is seen here at Sheffield Park on the Bluebell Railway.

Left: No. 847 in fine fettle as she climbs out of Horstead Keynes with her service.

Four-cylindered No. 850 *Lord Nelson* – the class which was designed to haul the heavy boat trains from London's Waterloo station to the Southampton Ocean Terminal. The class of sixteen were all named after naval commanders. The Southern bigwigs claimed that this engine was more powerful than anything the Great Western produced.

The GWR's response to the Southern Railway's claim that their engine was better was to produce the mighty 'King'. As much potential power as they could muster was put onto the frame of this 4-6-0. Thirty were built including this one, No. 6023 *King Edward II*, built in 1930 and seen here at the Didcot Railway Centre. The engine is resplendent in the short-lived livery of BR blue. (1949-1951).

Left: Looking splendid in authentic green livery, ex-LBSCR (IoW No. 8) *Freshwater* waits between shifts at Havenstreet.

Below: The Adams designed 0-4-4T '02' No. W24 *Calbourne* is awaiting a new running ticket and overhaul before returning to service. Here at Havenstreet on the Isle of Wight the engine sports a 1950 livery complete with the later BR crest.

Above: The SE&C pairing of 'C' Class No. 592 (BR 31592) and, Ashford built in 1905, 0-4-4 No. 263 wait for the guard's permission to take out the next northbound service from Horsted Keynes.

Right: Unrebuilt Bulleid 'Battle of Britain' Pacific 4-6-2 No. 34081 *92 Squadron* waits for her call of duty at the Nene Valley shed.

Above: Another unrebuilt Bulleid 'Battle of Britain' Pacific 4-6-2 No. 34067 *Tangmere* hurries along the West London Line on a sunny spring morning. SR No. 34067 (built 1947 at Brighton) is here heading a 'Golden Arrow Statesman' Pullman special to Canterbury and back.

Left: Rebuilt (with casing removed) Bulleid 'Merchant Navy' Pacific 4-6-2 No. 35028 *Clan Line* gets up to speed with the 'Lunchtime Special' Pullman from London's Victoria station. This class was the first to be built by Bulleid with Air-Smoothed casing – but later had it removed.

Another class of engine produced by Oliver Bulleid which also mostly had their casings removed. The Rebuilt 'Battle of Britain' Class No. 34059 *Sir Archibald Sinclair* runs into the station at Sheffield Park.

Deep in the West Country, 'Greyhound' 4-4-0 LSWR T9 No. 30120, a past stalwart of West Country passenger runs, now waits between services at the Bodmin General station, part of the preserved Bodmin & Wenford Railway. In 'blackberry' black BR livery, we note the early lion and wheel emblem on a high-capacity water carrying tender.

CHAPTER 5

GREAT WESTERN GLORY

No. 4965 *Rood Ashton Hall* heads her 'Shakespeare Express' train on a home run. The train thunders through Stratford Parkway heading for Birmingham's Snow Hill station.

Right: The Tyseley Loco Works holds an annual open day where they not only show off their special fleet but invite a few visitors too. First out onto the turntable is 'Hall' class 4965 *Rood Ashton Hall.*

Below: An enthralled crowd are in awe of this presentation of former 4-6-0 GWR engines. On the left is No. 7029 *Clun Castle* followed by 5043 *Earl of Mount Edgcumbe.* Then comes 'Castle' No. 5080 *Defiant* and 4965 *Rood Ashton Hall.*

Above: This picture shows Defiant without her name plate; the engine is in the final throes of her latest restoration. 4965 *Rood Ashton Hall* is coming forward onto the turntable.

Left: The Tyseley presenters do a great job in keeping everyone informed of the proceedings.

Above: Three Great Western engines stand together, all showing the Swindon heritage of succession and interchangeable parts. 'Castle' 4-6-0 No. 5080 *Defiant*, 4965 *Rood Ashton Hall* and new-build 'Grange' No. 6880 *Betton Grange* – (temporarily here as 6853). 4965 and 6880 both carry the same Swindon No. 4 boiler.

Right: The new-build 'Grange' No. 6880 *Betton Grange* shows its variations over the 'Halls'.

GWR 'Castle' class locomotive No. 5043 *Earl of Mount Edgcumbe* on the turntable at Tyseley. The highly successful class was being built right up until 1950 whilst many of her sister engines were being scrapped. This example was built in 1936 and is here seen in the BR express passenger livery of lined Brunswick green.

Standing together at the Tyseley station are '5700 Class' Pannier No. 9600 and LMS 'Jubilee' *Kolaphur.* No. 9600 carries the livery of BR lined black, that of express passenger engines.

Above: No. 9600 on a return trip with her train.

Right: Another post-war Great Western variation was the intro-duction of this more powerful Pannier Tank. The '9400' Class was the last of the Panniers to be introduced by Hawksworth. Built by the GWR (WR) between 1947 and 1956, here at Loughborough the powerful tapered-boiler engine (No. 9466) waits to take forward a postal special.

The well-travelled Port Talbot Railway 0-6-0ST No. 813 awaits in Bury Bolton St station for a call of duty.

In South Devon, running into Buckfastleigh station, is the Collett Goods mixed traffic engine No. 3205 which is the only survivor of a class of 120. Here she is sporting an unlined BR green livery.

With the 'stopping train' lamp headcode, GWR 'Manor' No. 7812 *Erlestoke Manor* runs into Bridgnorth station on the Severn Valley Railway with the Gresley rake of teak-bodied coaches.

WR 'Modified Hall' Class No. 6990 *Witherslack Hall* (built 1948) runs down the Great Central main line. The only stretch of main line on the preservation system.

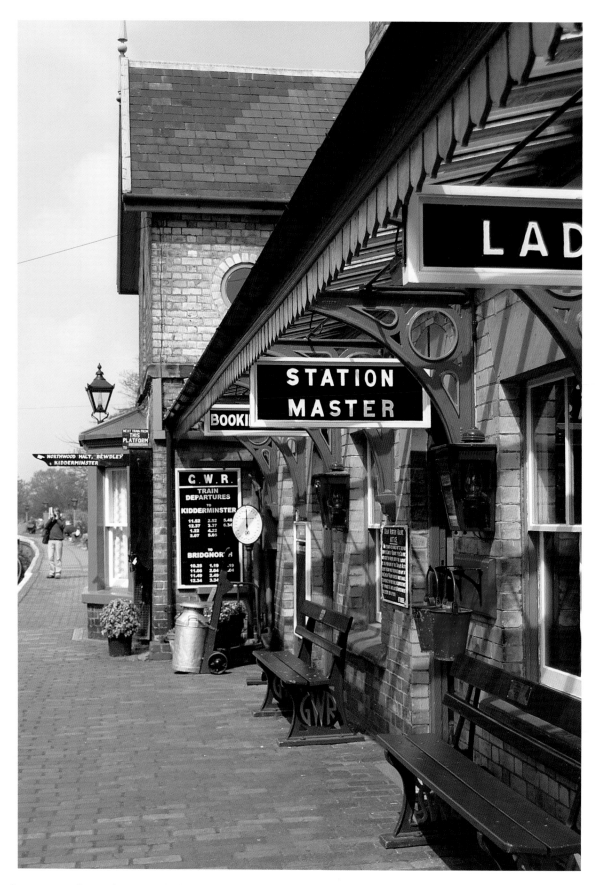

Arley, on the Severn Valley Railway, regularly wins awards. It is not hard to see why. The gardens and station buildings do it proud.

Above: Also on the Severn Valley is this scene at Kidderminster. 2-8-0 Class '2800' No. 2857 runs around its train. Rescued from Barry scrapyard in 1975, the engine was restored by a very dedicated group of enthusiasts.

Right: GWR Diesel Railcar on duty at Didcot. This class was loved by all, being produced when there was nothing like it around.

Left: Definitely GWR territory. The styles are similar, but that was always the Swindon policy – be interchangeable where possible. In the foreground is No. 5051 'Castle' class *Earl Bathurst*, with 5900 *Hinderton Hall* and 7808 *Cookham Manor* behind.

Below: King Edward has a running day at Didcot and is here waiting to back onto the demonstration line. As previously seen 'she' is of course No. 6023 *King Edward II*.

Two Great Western engines looking as though they fancy a run in the sunshine. 6023 *King Edward II* and No. 5051 'Castle' Class *Earl Bathurst*, who sometimes runs under her former name of *Drysllwyn Castle*. Both engines have wheel arrangements of 4-6-0 and have 4 cylinders. Note the end plates of the inside cylinders above the buffer beam.

CHAPTER 6

STREAMLINERS

A special day on the East Coast main line. 'A4' Class 60019 *Bittern* is seen in the guise of 4492 LNER *Dominion of New Zealand.* The train is getting up to speed at Holme crossing near Peterborough after taking water. This was the first time in over seventy years a Gresley 'A4' has had travelled this section of former Great Northern main line adorned in 'garter blue' with side valances attached.

60007 *Sir Nigel Gresley* waits at the level crossing at Grosmont before proceeding out of service. The ex-LNER 'A4' Pacific is in the short-lived (49/51) BR livery of blue given to engines of the designation 8P. Now though, it's not going to go away, for 'her' admirers love this livery.

Eastern Region liveried 4-6-2 No. 60009 *Union of South Africa* takes a turn at a preserved railway. Here she arrives at Wansford on the Nene Valley Railway.

Left: 'A4' at Bo'ness. No. 60007 LNER 'A4' Class 4-6-2 *Sir Nigel Gresley* occasionally tours the country and is here in Scotland.

Below: LMS Streamlined 'Duchess'. No. 6229 4-6-2 'Princess Coronation' class *Duchess of Hamilton* is depicted here in crimson lake livery at the National Railway Museum.

With the streamlining obsession of the thirties, everything seemed to succumb to streamlining. This picture shows that even the lamps got the treatment.

The only 'Duchess' running at present is un-streamlined LMS 'Coronation' Class 8P 4-6-2 No. 46233 *Duchess of Sutherland.* Here in crimson livery, she has arrived at her home base – the Midland Railway Centre at Butterley. This is an example of how the 'Duchess' looked after the streamlining had been removed.

Even the Great Western Railway attempted a bit of streamlining with the re-shaping of their 1930s diesel railcars.

Southern 'Battle of Britain' Class *92 Squadron* at Wansford on the Nene Valley Railway.

The culmination of a nine-day 'Great Britain VII' Railtour by RYTC. With the NRM in the background, LNER 4-6-2 No. 60009 *Union of South Africa* arrives ten minutes early at a cloudy York.

No. 60007 LNER 'A4' Class 4-6-2 *Sir Nigel Gresley* seen again in Scotland. The train is marshalled as a push-pull unit for the journey between Bo'ness and Manuel. Here the unit is moving out from Bo'ness with *Sir Nigel* taking up the rear.

CHAPTER 7

GREAT AT THE NENE

Above: BR No. 60163 *Tornado* is backing out of the shed area at Wansford on the Nene Valley Railway. Her badge commemorates the flying crews from the first Gulf war. Previously a badge was only added to this class if the name represented a pre-grouping railway company, eg 'Great Northern'.

Right: *Tornado* backs onto her train passing the 60-frame signalbox at Wansford. The British love affair with the steam engine is proved by the appearance of *Tornado*, built new from scratch by a set of very dedicated enthusiasts.

Left: New-build engine *Tornado* runs out of Wansford with an eastbound service.

Below: A great pair of locos to do a day's shift. Bulleid *92 Squadron* is passed by LMS 4-6-0 Stanier No. 6100 *Royal Scot*, again at the Nene Valley Railway.

'Battle of Britain' Class 92 *Squadron* moves out onto the running line at Wansford. The engine carries the favourite livery of designer Oliver Bulleid, malachite green.

The crew of LMS *Royal Scot* at the call into action at the Nene Valley Railway.

To the pleasure of many watchers, LMS *Royal Scot* powers out of Wansford station heading for Peterborough. The engine is in the BR livery of lined Brunswick Green.

CHAPTER 8

WARTIME AGAIN

Above: Standing by at the Haworth shed is US No. 5820, built in 1945 by Lima of Ohio to aid the war effort in Europe. The Worth Valley Railway found this example in Sweden.

Right: A study of a great wartime engine at the Great Central. Built at Ashford in 1943, LMS '8F' No. 48624 arrives at Leicester North.

Left: Two marvellous war engines, War Department No 90733 and USA Transportation Corps 'S160' 2-8-0 No. 5820 'Big Jim', sit together at Haworth. Both have the 2-8-0 wheel arrangement suited to the pulling of heavy trains.

Below: The engine shipped in from Ohio to aid the war effort. 'S160' 2-8-0 No. 5820 'Big Jim' is being prepared at the Haworth shed.

The Riddles designed wartime 'WD' Class. The 2-8-0 wheel arrangement Austerity locomotive 'WD' 90733 is showing the wartime livery of unlined matt black. It was built in January 1945 by The Vulcan Foundry Ltd for shipping to the continent.

No. 90775 backs off her train at Sheringham to run around the carriages. This is the larger Riddles 'WD' loco with a 2-10-0 wheel arrangement. This offers a wider route availability owing to the lighter axle load-ing. Of the ten coupled wheels, the centre pair are flangeless to enable sharper curves to be taken.

'WD' 2-10-0 90775 climbs the rise outside Sheringham station passing the golf course. A good test for any engine and crew.

The Riddles 'WD' 2-10-0 90775 hits the coast of north Norfolk. Built in 1943, the loco was part of a batch of 100 built by North British Locomotive Co. Glasgow. Ordered by the Ministry of Supply, the loco was shipped from new to the Middle East and ended up in Egypt. In 1945, along with fifteen sister locos, it was sold to Hellenic State Railways. The repatriation to the UK took place in August 1984.

Above: Switching tracks at Tenterden is SR 'USA' Class No 65. The shot gives a good view of the engine's very short wheelbase, one of the reasons for it being well suited for working the sharp curves around the former Southampton Dock lines.

Left: Part of the National Collection is the railway all-time ugly duckling. Designed by Bulleid in wartime, the brief was to cut all corners possible. He came up with the 'Q1' Class 0-6-0. This example is the only survivor numbered C1. It was the last class of this wheel arrangement to be built in Britain.

Left: USA Transportation Corps 'S160' 2-8-0 No. 5820 'Big Jim' departs Keighley for a run up the 330ft climb to Oxenhope on the Worth Valley Railway.

Below: LMS '8F' 2-8-0 No. 48624 powers along the racing stretch of the Great Central Railway with a demonstration goods. This is exactly what she was designed for during wartime, and was the Ministry of Supply's first choice of prime locomotive for war use.

Probably the greatest mixed-traffic engine of all time, LMS 'Black 5' 4-6-0 No. 45305 leaves Loughborough heading southbound to take the double-tracked section towards Leicester North.

When war was declared in 1939, the railways went into government control. The four big private companies which ran everything gave up their authority to the Ministry of Supply. That government department set about determining the needs of the country to go forward into the conflict with the need to prioritise the vital operations. Many old locomotives which were lined up for scrap were earmarked to be put back into use. Goods traffic would be the priority to cater for the huge troop and equipment movements. Immediately, all the streamlining of the Thirties was deemed frivolous and removed from engines where possible. The Ministry was aware of what happened in the previous war, and like then, chose an engine of the 2-8-0 wheel arrangement to be the ideal equipment to haul goods trains. The LMS '8F' was chosen for this purpose, whereby motions were set to build

more examples. A further 208 were constructed over the next couple of years for War Department use.

With the ever deepening of the war, the construction of these '8Fs' was proving to be more costly than the War Department would have liked. Also, they were taking considerable man hours to build, so plans were put in hand to simplify the situation. R.A. Riddles of the LMS was called in and asked to design a simplified version of the same engine to specifications laid down by the War Department; one that could pull a train of a 1,000 tons at 40mph. He was told that these must be as cheap and austere as possible, so much so that they need only to have a life of two to three years, after which they could be scrapped - or dumped in the sea, as Riddles did mention. Fabricated parts should be used wherever possible; everything needed to be simple to build and maintain. Other existing railway centres also needed to play their part with the building of three-and four-coupled types. Hunslet of Leeds took up the challenge here with their excellent austerity engines.

Riddles began designing the Austerities in 1942 to be built at various locations, the first examples appearing in January 1943. Each new engine was costed at £11,400, much less than for an '8F' and took 6,000 man hours fewer to build. Despite these economies, they were well received by drivers and firemen.

Soon after this, the Ministry of Supply wanted something else; an engine which could work over lightly laid track, or lines with weak bridges, with an axle loading of not more than thirteen tons. In other words, a powerful heavy freight engine, for use at home and abroad. Riddles came up with the 2-10-0, the first ever engine to be built in Britain with this wheel arrangement. This had a bigger boiler capable of producing more steam and again was an engine which might only have a lifespan of two years. Both types would be taken overseas to aid the movement of Allied troops and material after the invasion of Europe. They proved to be only slightly more expensive to build at £12,500 each and again were well received. The engine men and support workers were pleased with the new innovations such as a wide firebox and rocking grate for easy removal of the fire remains. One hundred and fifty were built, all at the Hyde Park Works, Glasgow. Some things, such as a tiny chimney and cast front wheels, are the first visual indicators of the spartan fittings used in the manufacture of these engines. These really do give them their 'utility' appearance. A feature of the 10-coupled wheel set are the flangeless centre wheels, as a large wheel arrangement like this would not be able to take tight curves. The removal of the centre flanges alleviates this problem. Also, the second and fourth driving wheels are shallow-flanged. Simplicity and ease of maintenance are the essential ingredients. Amazingly, while this was going on, the eccentric Oliver Bulleid of the Southern Railway was producing his air-smoothed Pacific engines. Supposedly produced as mixed-traffic engines, they were built with scant regard for using proven techniques which had ease of maintenance. All of Robert Riddles' engines, together with the '8F's, played an important part for the railways during and after the conflicts. So much so that Riddles was later asked to oversee the building of twelve new Standard Types after the railways became nationalised in 1948.

It shouldn't be forgotten the part women played in the running of the railways in wartime. Whereas in the First World War, women tended to fill the more unskilled roles left by the men going off to fight, this time their worth had been well recognised and a good many took up the more important roles which were essential to the smooth running of the system. Women now had equal voting rights to men and rightly knew the importance of the tasks they performed. Without the railways, the war could not have been won and without the women the railways could not have operated. After the war many more roles became available for them to fill. But it was not until 1958 that legislation was passed to offer equal pay to women who did equal jobs to men.

With the enemy continually targeting the railway system with bombs, it became very useful that so many routes across the country had been duplicated. So busy did some lines become with goods traffic, especially in the build up to D Day, that just about every siding or rail-loop would be filled with a train waiting for its passage. So intense were the workings that railway crews sometimes had to work all day and night. Engines would be a prime target for enemy fighter pilots, hence any gleaming metalwork, such as the brasswork on the GWR, would be painted black. Also, the side windows to the cabs would have the glass removed to be replaced with steel plate painted black.

It was not surprising then that line repair crews had to continually work on repairing damaged lines and had little time for anything else. By the end of it all, and when the systems were to be handed back to the private 'Big Four' companies, everything was in a very dilapidated state, so when the government offered those bosses compensation and a get-out chance they jumped at it.

KENT & LANCS DEFEND THE COUNTRY

1940s activity at the Kent & East Sussex Railway.

The Bluebell Railway gets into the act on the platform at Horsted Keynes station

All are prepared for war at the East Lancs Railway

AUSTERITY CONTINUES

ex-LNER 'K1' No. 62005 (which in the past has carried the name *Lord of the Isles*), collects water at Keighley station.

Above: 'B1' 4-6-0 No. 61264.
A Thompson post-war development which the LNER claimed performed easily as well as their rival Black 5. Here at Pickering in north Yorkshire, the loco has performed a season of service and has just brought a train into the station.

Right: 3 cylindered 'K4' Class No. 61994 *The Great Marquess* which was built with the Highlands Line in mind. It is seen here in service at the Worth Valley Railway.

Above: 'Modified Hall' Class No. 6990 4-6-0 *Witherslack Hall* prepares to run around its train at Leicester North station, the southern terminus of the Great Central Railway. Note the Hawksworth post-war flat sided tender.

Left: The Hawksworth pannier tank (1949) No. 1501 arrives at Holt station to complete the journey along the North Norfolk Railway.

Here on the turntable at Tyseley, the older 'Hall' shows some of the differences between the old and the newer 'Modified' type. This is *Rood Ashton Hall*. Apart from improved superheating, the newer type shows triangular stays above the buffer-beam and a strengthening cross-plate under the buffer beam between the bogies.

Ivatt Class '2' No. 41298 2-6-2T has been on the Isle of Wight since 2006 and has been fully restored. Designed by Ivatt, it is easy to see how this design influenced some of the later British Standard types.

The Ivatt Class '2' No. 41298 pulls away from Havenstreet, heading for Wootton. Not one of the carriages on this railway is less than seventy years old.

Another Bulleid 'Light Pacific' is at the Swanage Railway where we see 'Battle of Britain' class No. 34070 *Manston* being prepared by the turntable at Swanage.

Rebuilt 'Battle of Britain' Class No. 34059 *Sir Archibald Sinclair* runs into the station at Sheffield Park. Sir Archibald Sinclair was Wartime Secretary of State for Air. This shows the look of the engine after the casing (see previous picture) has been removed.

Left: 'B12' No. 8572 has taken water and prepares to take the next service out of Sheringham.

Below: The 'B12' in action after leaving Sheringham. No. 8572 (BR 61572) attacks the grade out beside the golf course.

Above: London Midland and Scottish Railway Class Five (Black 5) 4-6-0 No. 45305 leaves Loughborough heading southward. The Great Central Railway loco heads the train towards the double-tracked main line section. Built by Armstrong Whitworth in 1937, No. 45305 was withdrawn from active service in 1968.

Right: The distinctive lines of double-chimneyed rebuilt 4-6-0 Stanier No. 6100 *Royal Scot* at Minehead. This engine was formerly No. 6152 *The King's Dragoon Guardsman*; the identity was changed before the US trip in 1933 but never changed back.

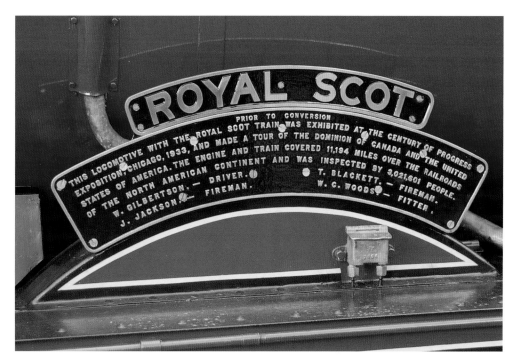

Left: The nameplate of *Royal Scot* tells us of that visit to Canada and USA in 1933.

Below: Sporting a new livery of BR Brunswick green, now as BR No. 46100, 4-6-0, *Royal Scot* runs forward at Wansford to start a special day on the Nene Valley Railway.

Right: The interior of a carriage of the 'Chesham' set at the Bluebell Railway gives an indication of the conditions to which suburban travellers would have been subjected.

Below: The work roster of the Sheffield Park shed shows some very proud names.

TURN	LOCO	DRIVER	FIREMAN	CLEANER
11	80151	A. WILKENS	G. HARPER	
12	34059	M. LEE	B. COUGHLAN	J. THOMSON
13	80151	B. SMITH	K. UPTON	
14	9017	C. GROOME	M. WILLIAMS	
16	34059	W. WHITE	D. TOMSETT	
X		C. HUNFORD	J. BRYANT	D. FRENCH
RF		L. NODES		L K. SULLIVAN
C		R. MILLARD	J. BARTON	

CHAPTER 11

BRITISH STANDARD LOCOS

Left: LMS Ivatt 2-6-0 No. 46521 shows where Robert Riddles took his inspiration when designing the British Standard Class '2' engines. Here running southbound on the GCR.

Below: BR Standard Class '2' 2MT 2-6-0 (Mogul) No.78019 prepares to take a stopping train along the Great Central Main Line. This class is a derivation of the Ivatt '46400' types, which were so successful an innovation after the war.

British Standard '4' tank engine No. 80072 is the guest engine on this day in Kent. Usually located at the Llangollen Railway, the engine formerly worked on the suburban services out of Fenchurch Street station, London.

Another BS Class '4' tank engine is No. 80136, here seen on passenger duty at the Great Central Railway.

Left: The inspiration for the BS Class '2', Ivatt No. 41298 2-6-2T running around at Smallbrook Junction, the eastern end of the Isle of Wight Steam Railway.

Below: BS Class '4' 2-6-0 No.76084 switches platforms at Sheringham. Beyond the level crossing the national network begins, with the next station being Cromer. North Norfolk now has excellent railway connections for tourists.

Along the line which touches the coast of North Norfolk, BR Class '4' 2-6-0 No. 76084 heads westbound towards Weybourne.

No. 73050 *City of Peterborough* prepares to take the next service out of Wansford station on the Nene Valley Railway. This railway uses extensive Continental coaching stock, giving them a good advantage when a film company needs a foreign scene. The BR Standard '5' 4-6-0 was built in 1954 at Derby. This was a class designed to supersede the Black 5s.

Left: BR 'Britannia' Class No. 70013 *Oliver Cromwell* in the preparation area at Loughborough. The 'Britannias' were the flagship locomotives of the British Standard range, with No. 70004 *William Shakespeare* being exhibited at the Festival of Britain on London's South Bank in 1951.

Below: The engine which hauled the famous 15 guinea special at the end of steam in 1968, hence ensuring its survival. BR 'Britannia' Class No. 70013 *Oliver Cromwell* pulls off her train at Oxenhope at the end of the Worth Valley Railway (K&WVR). Fifty-five of this class were built.

Above: The locomotive which artist David Shepherd bought direct from BR at the end of steam, seen here at Toddington on the Gloucestershire Warwickshire Railway '9F' 2-10-0 No. 92203 *Black Prince* stands in preparation for her next turn of duty.

Right: Now resident at the North Norfolk Railway, '9F' 2-10-0 No. 92203 *Black Prince* powers into action departing Weybourne.

Left: The huge 2-10-0 wheel arrangement of '9F' No. 92203 *Black Prince* stands out prominently as the engine prepares to depart from Sheringham.

Below: BR 'Standard' Class No. 71000 *Duke of Gloucester* approaches Highley station from the south on the Severn Valley Railway.

Right: At the end of the journey at Bridgnorth, the impressive BS engine No.71000 *Duke of Gloucester* rests in the evening sunlight. The high running plate shows the typical styling of the British 'Standard' classes.

Below: BR 'Standard' Class No. 71000 *Duke of Gloucester* approaches Hampton Loade station from the south on the Severn Valley Railway. This engine was built as a solitary class of one.

From where the railways were after the war, it was no surprise that they became public property, with nationalisation. The owners of the Big Four railway companies, who had briefly had their control reinstated after the government control of wartime, had no hesitation in taking a pay-off and getting out. Instead of there being four regionalised private companies, the railways would continue with the same regions but now they were to be called Eastern Region, Southern Region, Western Region and Midland Region under public ownership. There would also be a North Eastern and Scottish Region.

As has been previously described, the Big Four had attempted to redress the shortcomings of the locomotive stock which was handed back to them. The GWR built Castles, Halls and Manors. The LNER came along with 'A1s', 'A2s', 'B1s', 'B2s', etc. with the Southern moving ahead with Bulleid and his 'air-smoothed' Pacifics.

After nationalisation in 1948, the new regional regimes were allowed for a short time to maintain the liveries from the old Big Four, the only difference being that it was British Railways spelled out on the tenders and not the old logos. It is good to see that many examples of these liveries appear on locos in the age of preservation. By the turn of the next decade, BR had standardised all liveries with generally 'blackberry black' becoming the most common with the lion and wheel logo.

After the hostilities, all the failings of a wartime regime would come to light. There would have been minimal works on reinstating worn out track, following a wartime necessity of only repairing track which had been damaged, with the strong priorities of wartime being that of maintaining goods traffic. There was therefore a big shortage of suitable locomotives for passenger trains and there was still a glut of smaller engines from pre-grouping days which now needed to be replaced as soon as possible.

George Ivatt of the LMS was probably the most innovative main man of this period, for he introduced the classes of tank and tender engines which attained the nickname of 'Mickey Mouse' engines. This comment came from the railwaymen owing to the fragility of their appearance. But very successful they were, which not only led to the removal of worn out engines from the system, but his ideas and engines, with small modifications, were taken up by Robert Riddles to become standard types.

The power classification for the new BS classes was taken straight from the old LMS, as it would be with Robert Riddles formerly in charge of the LMS. He had become in all but name the Chief Mechanical Engineer hired by the newly formed British Railways to oversee the design and construction of these new types. The power classifications started with the lowest being 'one' and going through to the most powerful which would be 'nine' – and all types were required.

The general formation of the new British Standard Types were as follows:

1. 84xxx Class '2', 2-6-2T, based on Ivatt Class '2' tank. 30 built – None Preserved.
   New example being created at Bluebell Railway using 78059 as a donor.
2. 82xxx Class '3', 2-6-2T, tank version of the 77xxx type, 45 built.
   None Preserved. New-build in progress at Severn Valley Railway.
3. 78xxx Class '2', 2-6-0, Standard Ivatt Class '2' type. 65 built.
   Five in Preservation.
4. 80xxx Class '4', 2-6-4T, the well-liked Fowler/Stanier/Fairburn/Ivatt style continued. 155 built.
   Fifteen in Preservation.
5. 77xxx Class '3', 2-6-0, for lightly laid routes. 20 built.
   All extinct.
6. 76xxx Class '4', 2-6-0, based on the heavier Ivatt Class '4'. 115 built.
   Four in Preservation. Note the tender which incorporates a back for the cab.
7. 75xxx Class '4', 4-6-0. Introduced to replace the 'Manor' Class of the GWR with the Cambrian Coast route in mind. 80 built.
   Six survive in Preservation.
8. Class '5', 73xxx 4-6-0, designed to compliment the 'Black 5s' of the LMS. 172 built. Nos. 73125-73154 had Caprotti valve-gear fitted.
   Five in Preservation.
9. Class '6', 72xxx 'Clan', 4-6-2, a lighter version of the 'Britannia'. Ten built (used mostly in Scotland). None survived.
   One new-build under construction. No. 72010 'Hengist'.

10. The 70xxx 'Britannia', 4-6-2 (two-cylinder) Class. 55 built.

    Two Preserved, 70000 *Britannia* and 70013 *Oliver Cromwell*.

11. The 71xxx, 4-6-2 (just one example which is preserved). No. 71000 *Duke of Gloucester*.

    Probably the finest achievement for the preservationists.

12. '9F' 92xxx 2-10-0 built for heavy freight but also used for passenger services. 251 built. Nine survive in Preservation.

The boy train-spotters of the Fifties were not particularly impressed with the 'Standard' Types; not being linked to a particular region there could be no taking sides with them. The '9Fs' impressed but that was about all. Everyone had their 'Region' and that was it. The last engine of all time in Britain was '9F' *Evening Star* coming out of Swindon in 1960. This is amazing because in 1955, the British Transport Commission had formulated a 'Modernisation Plan' announcing the intention to move to electric and diesel traction within the shortest time possible. All steam was to be removed from the tracks of Britain's railways.

It was so obvious to all that steam was nearing the end. The planning of railways had not properly taken into account of how the roads were largely to take away the freight traffic. Huge marshalling yards had been planned and installed in the late Fifties, all to become a shadow of themselves within a few years. Orders had been placed for the standard types of engines, so much so that finally 999 examples were produced. All the stock ran in a state of increasing grime. Very few boys wanted to come into a business which was so obviously dying. The cleaning of engines had, by the reality of the situation, become a thing of the past.

These last locomotives coming out of the workshops ended up having a ridiculously short life, sometimes six to eight years. The normal lifespan for an engine would be at least twenty to thirty years.

The British Transport Commission responded to a government demand to take some drastic action. They did this by employing an outside consultant with the essential business and industrial skills – Dr. Richard Beeching, at the time on the board of ICI, the giant pharmaceutical corporation, but, after some localised surveys, he went about ruthlessly formulating what was to become the Beeching Report.

His recommendations stated that over 200 branch lines should be closed, with the removal of some 2,000 stations and 5,000 miles of track. Little heed was placed to the plight of remote areas and the devastation to services which might occur. Any objections were scantly reviewed and rejected - the country was in shock. The railways went forward and became more efficient, but without initially becoming profitable.

The shockwaves of it all did result in one particular upside. The railway enthusiasts who had witnessed the last rites of steam in this country suddenly noticed something. Those branch lines which had been so ruthlessly abandoned still stood there with no particular purpose. The cleverest of people took the opportunity to open some of those as heritage steam railways. The authorities must themselves been still in some sort of shock, because they largely agreed. The seeds were sown, and forty years later we have over a hundred such centres operating, an achievement which is beyond comprehension. The public, though, do show their thanks and approval by attending and supporting in huge numbers.

CHAPTER 12

PRESERVATION RULES

GREAT GOODS

Wartime 'Q1' Class 0-6-0 No. C1 is showing her versatility. At Sheffield Park on the Bluebell Railway, the engine hauls a goods train through Sheffield Park station.

Above: Pulling a double-length goods train is the Riddles duo of BR 4MT 2-6-4T No. 80136 and 2MT 2-6-0 No. 78018. The train is passing Woodthorp where on the left a new housing development is taking place.

Right: On a special day when the Isle of Wight Steam Railway celebrates goods traffic, a 'Terrier' engine runs past with a display of renovated trucks.

The smaller driving wheels of the LMS '8F' loco clearly show that she was built for power and not speed. 2-8-0 No. 48624 heads a demonstration goods southward from Loughborough.

With the sea in the background, Pannier Tank engine No. 7714 takes out a modest goods train along the North Norfolk Railway.

Some authentic loose coupled shunting can be seen and heard at the Midland Railway Centre. Here it is all happening at Swanwick station.

8F Midland Region 2-8-0 No. 48624 in an alternative crimson livery, doing what she loved to do – haul freight trains. This mineral rake powers away from Loughborough along the GCR double track section.

GREAT PAIRINGS

Above: BR 4MT 2-6-4T No. 80136 is at the Great Central Railway's 'Goods Galore' weekend. Here the tank loco is piloting another visitor, this time from the NYMR: 2MT 2-6-0 No. 78018.

Left: The GWR Panniers No. 9600 and 7752 (L94) make a departure from their Tyseley base to take a 'Pannier Rambler' Railtour around the Midlands. Here the pair are at full-tilt coming through Kidderminster where they give a whistle salute to the nearby Severn Valley Railway.

The spectacular SE&CR pairing get underway at Horsted Keynes. Ashford built 0-4-4T No. 263 pilots 'C' Class No. 592 (BR 31592).

The rare pairing of two engines with their roots in Victorian times. *City of Truro* coupled with *Earl of Berkeley* double-head a service out of Ropley arriving from Alresford.

'Black 5' No. 45231 *The Sherwood Forester* pilots the rebuilt 'West Country' Class No. 34046 *Braunton* as the train proceeds along the West Somerset Railway. The double-header turns into a southerly direction having left Williton to head towards Bishops Lydeard.

This time the same combination as before are heading in a westerly direction towards Minehead; 'Black 5' No. 45231 *The Sherwood Forester* and 'West Country' light Pacific No. 34046 *Braunton*.

Right: A visitor to the North Norfolk's autumn steam gala is GWR Collett '57xx' class 0-6-0PT 7714. Passing the golf course outside Sheringham, the Pannier Tank is piloting S&DJR 7F 53809, on loan from the West Somerset Railway.

Below: A great pairing at the Nene Valley Railway. Bulleid 92 *Squadron* is passed by LMS 4-6-0 Stanier No. 6100 *Royal Scot*.

We have seen them in Sheringham station, but here they are out in the open country; the GNR & LNER pairing of Nos.1744 & 8572 approach the A149 heading towards Weybourne.

Class '4' No. 76084 heads the Somerset & Dorset 7F 2-8-0 No. 53809 powering across the A149 road bridge.

RETURN TO THE MET

On the special 'Steam Back on the Met' event, electric unit *Sarah Siddons* comes out of the tunnel at Farringdon station bound for Hammersmith. These electric units ran between Baker Street and the outer reaches of Metroland from 1923 until their withdrawal in 1962.

Above: London Transport-liveried GWR small prairie 2-6-2T No. 5521 (with the reduced cab), running as L150, heads the train as it departs Rickmansworth heading for Chesham. No. 12 *Sarah Siddons* is not required for motive power on this occasion. The electric locomotive being absolutely at home on her former running ground at Rickmansworth.

Left: '57xx' 0-6-0PT (GWR 7715) No. L99 was part of a batch sold to London Transport between 1956 and 1963. Here on the Spa Valley Railway, the Pannier is resplendent in LT colours. It was L94 (now resident at Tyseley) which hauled a last train out of Farringdon station on 6 June 1971 to effectively end all network steam activity in Britain.

London Transport now needs Class 20 diesel locos to provide air braking facilities for their 4TC suburban coaching stock. No. 20142 is one of the pair providing this. The loco carries the LT livery and is named *Sir John Betjeman*.

Metropolitan 'E' Class Locomotive No. 1, 0-4-4T, is the star on any running on the Met. No. 1 worked the last steam train on the Chesham branch in 1960, but is here about to leave Hammersmith. The carriage behind the engine is Metropolitan milk van No. 3, which dates from 1896.

At the western end of the line and in bright daylight, electric Bo-Bo No. 12 is at the buffers of Hammersmith station.

ON THE MAIN

Standard 'Britannia' Class 4-6-2 No. 70013 *Oliver Cromwell* is on the former Great Eastern line between London's Liverpool Street station and Norwich. Here she is on the return leg at Colchester. The engine is famous for helping run the last steam rail tour in August 1968, known as the 'Fifteen Guinea Special'.

Above: 'Shakespeare Express' approaches Moor Street station, headed by GWR 'Castle' Class locomotive No. 5043 *Earl of Mount Edgcumbe.*

Right: No. 4965 *Rood Ashton Hall* hurries through Stratford Parkway. No. 4965 was built at Swindon in 1929. The Collett designed mixed traffic engine was a product of Swindon succession.

No. 46233 'Coronation' Pacific *Duchess of Sutherland* pulls away southwards from Peterborough heading for London's King's Cross station.

On the West Highland Line in Scotland, LNER 'K1' 2-6-0 No. 62005 crosses the curving Glenfinnan Viaduct. An innovative structure when built using un-reinforced concrete.

Above: A3 4-6-2 (Pacific) No. 60103 *Flying Scotsman* passes Conington on the inaugural re-launch after renovation along the East Coast main line, 25 February 2016. The record-breaking Gresley masterpiece has the later styling of German type smoke deflectors and double chimney.

Right: Despite their unpopularity with enthusiasts – as they were part of the steam replacement programme – the Diesel Multiple Unit trains gave a view like no other; from a seat behind the driver the whole of the view ahead can be seen. This is the Great Central main line.

Left: Rebuilt Bulleid 'Merchant Navy' Pacific 4-6-2 No. 35028 *Clan Line* prepares to take out the 'Lunchtime Special' Pullman from London's Victoria station. This class was the first to be built by Bulleid with air-smoothed casing. The first came into use in 1941 painted in unlined matt black, with names and a Malachite green colour scheme being added after the hostilities. Here the engine is finished in BR express passenger lined Brunswick green.

Below: The names of the 'Merchant Navy' Class were given to commemorate the merchant shipping lines who were involved in the Battle of the Atlantic and who used the Southampton Docks. Here, No. 35028 picks up a good rhythm as she heads to cross the Thames. The iconic Battersea Power Station is in the distance.

A total of thirty 'Merchant Navy' Class engines were built, of which eleven survive into preservation, but not all have yet been restored. No. 35028 *Clan Line* had the good fortune to be sold into private ownership straight from British Railways in 1967, so has never required massive rebuilding. Here the train makes the river crossing as seen from Chelsea Bridge.

The 'Lunchtime Special' arrives at Clapham Junction before taking a circular route, allowing the customers to have a special dining experience. All of this class originally had the Air Smoothed (streamlined) casing and all were rebuilt in the late fifties to have it removed, unlike some of the similar preserved 'Light Pacifics' which remained original.

No. 6023 *King Edward II* powers along the Great Central racing stretch of main line double trackwork.

LMS 5MT 4-6-0 No. 45407 *The Lancashire Fusilier* is about to take the 'Royal Duchy' train on a steam tour to Cornwall and back from Bristol. Here the train is ready to depart from Temple Meads station.

THE MET AGAIN

Class 20 diesels arrived in the late fifties and were a revelation – especially to signalmen. Their acceleration was very impressive. The vision for the driver is poor when going forwards but excellent the other way, so that's the way they generally go. The Met Special is here travelling through Chalfont and Latimer.

Above: Running in reverse, Metropolitan No. 1 is tethered to 'chunky' Pannier No.9466 and Class 20 diesel No. 20142. Class 20 No. 20227 at the far end. Impressive motive power for just four carriages.

Left: The constable on Amersham station shows how policing used to be.

STEAM GUIDE (STANDARD GAUGE)

ALDERNEY RAILWAY
Alderney. C.I.
www.alderneyrailway.com
Tel: 01455 634373

AVON VALLEY RAILWAY
Bitton Station. Nr. Bristol. 6HD
www.avonvalleyrailway.org.uk
Tel: 01457 484950

BARROW HILL ROUNDHOUSE
Chesterfield. Derbyshire. S43 2PR
www.barrowhill.org.uk
Tel: 01246 472450

BARRY TOURIST RAILWAY
www.barrytouristrailway.co.uk
Tel: 01446748816

BATTLEFIELD LINE RAILWAY
Shackerstone Epping Ongar. CV13 6NW
www.battlefield-line-railway.co.uk
Tel: 01827 880754

BLUEBELL RAILWAY
Sheffield Park Station. TN22 3QL
Horsted Keynes Station. RH17 7BB
www.bluebell-railway.co.uk
Tel: 01825 720800

BODMIN AND WENFORD RAILWAY
Bodmin General Station. PL31 1AQ
www.bodminrailway.co.uk
Tel: 01208 73666

BO'NESS AND KINNEIL RAILWAY
Bo'ness Station. EH51 9AQ
www.bkrailway.co.uk
Tel: 01506 825855

BOWES RAILWAY CENTRE
Gateshead. NE9 7QJ

www.newcastlegateshead.com
Tel: 01914 161847

BRESSINGHAM STEAM MUSEUM
Nr. Diss. Norfolk. IP22 2AA
www.bressingham.co.uk
Tel: 01379 686900

BRISTOL HARBOUR RAILWAY
Princes Wharf. BS1 4RN
www.bristolharbourrailway.co.uk
Tel: 01173 526600

BUCKINGHAMSHIRE RAILWAY CENTRE
Quainton Road Station. HP22 4BY
www.bucksrailcentre.org.uk
Tel: 01296 655720

CALEDONIAN RAILWAY
Brechin Station. DD9 7AF
www.caledonian-railway.com
Tel: 01356 622992

CHASEWATER RAILWAY
Brownhills West. WS8 7NL
www.chasewaterrailway.co.uk
Tel: 01543 452623

CHINNOR & PRINCES RISBOROUGH
RAILWAY
Chinnor Station. OX39 4ER
www.chinnorrailway.co.uk
Talking Timetable: 01844 353535

CHOLSEY & WALLINGFORD RAILWAY
Wallingford. OX10 9GQ
www.cholsey-wallingford-railway.com
Tel: 01491 835067

CHURNET VALLEY RAILWAY
Kingsley & Froghall Station. ST10 2HA
www.churnet-valley-railway.org.uk

Tel: 01538 750755

COLNE VALLEY RAILWAY
Castle Hedingham. CO9 3DZ
www.colnevalleyrailway.co.uk
Tel: 01787 461174

DARLINGTON RAILWAY MUSEUM
Station Rd. Darlington. DL3 6ST
www.darlington.gov.uk
Tel: 01325 460532

DARTMOOR RAILWAY
Okehampton. EX20 1EJ
www.dartmoorrailway.com
Tel: 01837 55164

DARTMOUTH STEAM RAILWAY &
RIVER BOAT COMPANY
Paignton. TQ4 6AF
www.dartmouthrailriver.co.uk
Tel: 01803 555872

DEAN FOREST RAILWAY
Lydney. GL15 4ET
www.deanforestrailway.co.uk
Tel: 01594 845840

DERWENT VALLEY LIGHT RAILWAY
Murton Park, York. YO19 5UF
www.dvlr.org.uk
Tel: 01904 489966

DIDCOT RAILWAY CENTRE
Didcot. OX11 7NJ
www.didcotrailwaycentre.org.uk
Tel: 01235 817200

DOWNPATRICK & Co. DOWN RAILWAY
Downpatrick Station. N.I. BT30 6LZ
www.downrail.co.uk
Tel: 02844 612233

EAST ANGLIAN RAILWAY MUSEUM
Chappel, Near Colchester. CO6 2DS
www.earm.co.uk
Tel: 01206 242524

EAST KENT RAILWAY
Shepherdswell. CT15 7PD
www.eastkentrailway.co.uk
Tel: 01304 832042

EAST SOMERSET RAILWAY
Cranmore Station. BA4 4QP
www.eastsomersetrailway.co.uk
Tel: 01749 880417

EAST LANCASHIRE RAILWAY
Bury Bolton Street Station. BL9 0EY
Rawtenstall Station. BB4 6DD
Ramsbottom Station. BL0 9AL
www.eastlancsrailway.org.uk
Tel: 01617 647790

ECCLESBOURNE VALLEY RAILWAY
Wicksworth. DE4 4FB
www.e-v-r.com
Tel: 01629 823076

ELSECAR HERITAGE RAILWAY
Elscar Heritage Centre. S74 8HJ
www.elsecarrailway.co.uk
Tel: 01226 740203

EMBSAY & BOLTON ABBEY STEAM
RAILWAY
Bolton Abbey Station, Skipton. BD23 6AF.
www.embsayboltonabbeyrailway.org.uk
Tel: 01756 710614
Talking Timetable: 01756 795189

EPPING-ONGAR: RAILWAY
Ongar Town. CM5 9AB
www.eorailway.co.uk
Tel: 01277 365200

FOXFIELD STEAM RAILWAY
Blythe Bridge. ST11 9BG
www.foxfieldrailway.co.uk
Tel: 01782 396210

GLOUCESTERSHIRE WARWICKSHIRE
RAILWAY
Toddington Station. GL54 5DT

Winchcombe Station. GL54 5LB
www.gwsr.com
Tel: 01242 621405

GREAT CENTRAL RAILWAY
Loughborough Central Station. LE11 1RW
Quorn & Woodhouse. LE12 8AW
Leicester North. LE4 3BR
www.gcrailway.co.uk
Tel: 01509 632323

GT CENTRAL-NOTTINGHAM
Ruddington. NG11 6JS
www.gcrn.co.uk
Tel: 0115 9405705

GWILI RAILWAY
Carmarthen. SA33 6HT
www.gwili-railway.co.uk
Tel: 01267 230666

GWR (Steam Museum)
Swindon. SN2 2EY
www.steam-museum.org.uk
Tel: 01793 466646

ISLE OF WIGHT STEAM RAILWAY
Havenstreet. PO33 4DS
www.iwsteamrailway.co.uk
Tel: 01983 882204

KEIGHLEY & WORTH VALLEY
RAILWAY
Haworth Station. BD22 8NJ
Keighley Station. BD21 4HP
www.kwvr.co.uk
Tel: 01535 645214

KENT AND EAST SUSSEX RAILWAY
Tenterden Station. TN30 6HE
www.kesr.org.uk
Tel: 01580 765155.
Talking Timetable: 01580 762943

LAKESIDE & HAVERTHWAITE
 RAILWAY
Haverthwaite Station. LA12 8AL

www.lakesiderailway.co.uk
Tel: 01539 531594

LAVENDER LINE
Isfield Station. TN22 5XB
www.lavender-line.co.uk
Tel: 01825 750515

LINCOLNSHIRE WOLDS RAILWAY
Ludborough. DN36 5SH
www.lincolnshirewoldsrailway.co.uk
Tel: 01507 363881

LLANGOLLEN RAILWAY
Llangollen Station. LL20 8SN
www.llangollen-railway.co.uk
Tel: 01978 860979

MANGAPPS FARM RAILWAY MUSEUM
Burnham-on-Crouch. CM0 8QG
www.mangapps.co.uk
Tel: 01621 784898

MIDDLETON RAILWAY
Hunslet. LS10 2JQ
www.middletonrailway.org.uk
Tel: 0845 680 1758

MID-NORFOLK RAILWAY
Dereham Station. NR19 1DF
www.mnr.org.uk
Tel: 01362 851723

MID HANTS RAILWAY (WATERCRESS LINE)
Railway Station Alresford. SO24 9JG
Ropley Station. SO24 0BL
www.watercressline.co.uk
Tel: 01962 733810

MIDLAND RAILWAY CENTRE
Butterley Station. DE5 3QZ
Swanwick Junction.
www.midlandrailwaycentre.co.uk
Tel: 01773 570140

MID-SUFFOLK LIGHT RAILWAY
Wetheringsett. IP14 5PW

www.mslr.org.uk
Tel: 01449 766899

NATIONAL RAILWAY MUSEUM
Leeman Road. York. YO26 4XL
www.nrm.org.uk
Tel: 08448 153139

NENE VALLEY RAILWAY
Wansford Station. PE8 6LR
www.nvr.org.uk
Tel: 01780 784444

NORTHAMPTON & LAMPORT
RAILWAY
Pitsford & Brampton Station. NN6 8BA
www.nlr.org.uk
Tel: 01604 820327

NORTHAMPTONSHIRE IRONSIDE
RAILWAY TRUST
Northampton. NN4 9UW
www.nirt.co.uk
Tel: 01604 702031

NORTH NORFOLK RAILWAY
Sheringham Station. NR26 8RA
Holt Station. NR25 6AJ
www.nnrailway.co.uk
Tel: 01263 820800

NORTH TYNESIDE STEAM RAILWAY
(Stephenson Railway Museum)
North Shields. NE29 8DX
www.twmuseums.org.uk

NORTH YORKSHIRE MOORS RAILWAY
Pickering. YO18 7AJ
Goathland. YO22 5NF
Grosmont. YO22 5QE
www.nymr.co.uk
Tel: 01751 472508

PALLOT STEAM, MOTOR &
GENERAL MUSEUM
Jersey. C.I.

www.pallotmuseum.co.uk
Tel: 01534 865307

PEAK RAIL
Matlock. DE4 3NA
www.peakrail.co.uk
Tel: 01629 580381

PLYM VALLEY RAILWAY
Plympton. PL7 4NW
www.plymrail.co.uk

PONTYPOOL & BLAENAVON
RAILWAY
Blaenavon. NP4 9ND
www.pontypool-and-blaenavon.co.uk
Tel: 01495 792263

RAILWAY PRESERVATION
SOCIETY OF IRELAND
www.steamtrainsireland.com

RUTLAND RAILWAY MUSEUM
Cottesmore. LE15 7BX
www.rutnet.co.uk
Tel: 01572 813203

SEVERN VALLEY RAILWAY
Bridgnorth. WV16 5DT
Bewdley. DY12 1BG
Kidderminster. DY10 1QX
www.svr.co.uk
Tel: 01299 403816

SOUTH DEVON RAILWAY
Buckfastleigh. TQ11 0DZ
www.southdevonrailway.co.uk
Tel: 08433 571420

SOUTHALL RAILWAY CENTRE
Southall. UB2 4SE
www.gwrpg.co.uk
Tel: 0208 574 1529

SPA VALLEY RAILWAY
Tunbridge Wells. TN2 5QY

www.spavalleyrailway.co.uk
Tel: 01892 537715

STRATHSPEY RAILWAY
Aviemore. PH22 1PY
www.strathspeyrailway.co.uk
Tel: 01479 810725

SWANAGE RAILWAY
Swanage. BH19 1HB
www.swanagerailway.co.uk
Tel: 01929 425800

SWINDON & CRICKSLADE STEAM
RAILWAY
Blunsdon. Wilts.
www.swindon-crickslade-railway.org.uk
Tel: 01793 771615

TANFIELD RAILWAY
Gateshead. NE16 5ET

www.tanfield-railway.co.uk
Tel: 0845 463 4938

TELFORD STEAM RAILWAY
Horsehay. TF4 2NG
www.telfordsteamrailway.co.uk

TYSELEY RAILWAY CENTRE
670 Warwick Road. Tyseley. B11 2HL
www.tyseleylocoworks.co.uk
Vintage Trains: 01217 084960

WEST SOMERSET RAILWAY
Minehead Station. TA24 5BG
Williton Station. TA4 4RQ
Bishops Lydeard. TA4 3RU
www.westsomersetrailway.co.uk
Tel: 01643 704996

INDEX